Any Holy City

The Gerald Cable Book Award Series

Love Fugue
Shulamith Wechter Caine

Dime Store Erotics
Ann Townsend

Bodies that Hum
Beth Gylys

Inventing Difficulty
Jessica Greenbaum

Why They Grow Wings
Nin Andrews

Odd Botany
Thorpe Moeckel

A Parade of Hands
James Hoch

Lime
Audrey Bohanan

Any Holy City

Mark Conway

Silverfish Review Press

ACKNOWLEDGMENTS

Thanks to the editors of the following publications in which some of these poems, sometimes in a slightly different version, first appeared: *Agni, Bomb, Boston Review, Columbia: A Journal of Literature and Art, The Cresset, Drunken Boat, Florida Review, Fuori, The Gettysburg Review, Grolier Poetry Prize Annual, Harvard Review, The Journal, The Laurel Review, The Paris Review, Ploughshares, Prairie Schooner,* and *Slate.*

"Before I Begin" and "Coming In" were reprinted in *Swerve* and "The Left Bank" was reprinted in *Verse Daily.* "After Abraham Mourns, He Requests Another Son" along with a number of the above poems appeared in a chapbook (*First Body*) which won the 2003 Aldrich Poetry Competition, selected by Robert Pinsky.

Thanks are due to so many for improving these poems and this book – I'm very grateful to Marie Howe, Nick Flynn, Jeff Shotts, John Ruff, Anne McCarty, Jason Shinder, April Bernard, David Lehman, Lucie Brock-Broido, Donald Hall, Kate Moos, John Welle, Mark McKeon, Sheridan Reilly, Cindy Malone, Robert Pinsky, Li-Young Lee, Jaime Clark, Mike Rosovsky, Victoria Redel, Carl Phillips, Alan Reed, Joe O'Connell, all my family, my wife, Therese Nierengarten and my large-hearted and strong-greaved sons, Samuel, Cullen and Liam Conway. Significant help arrived from the Corporation of Yaddo, the Loft Literary Center, the McKnight Foundation, the Minnesota State Arts Board, the Jerome Foundation, SASE, the Ragdale Foundation, the Blacklock Nature Sanctuary, the Central Minnesota Arts Board, Bread Load Writers Conference and the Aldrich Contemporary Art Museum. Special thanks to Rodger Moody; and in memory of my mother, D.A.

Copyright © 2005 by Silverfish Review Press

Published by Silverfish Review Press
P.O. Box 3541
Eugene, OR 97403

ISBN: 1-878851-22-5

Publication of this book was made possible in part by a generous grant from Literary Arts of Portland, Oregon.

All rights reserved.
Except by a reviewer, no part of this book may be reproduced or utilized in any form or by any means, electronic or mechanical, including photocopying and recording, without permission in writing from the publisher.

Cover art: Original San Francisco Earthquake postcard.
Cover design by Valerie Brewster, Scribe Typography.
Text design by Rodger Moody and Connie Kudura, ProtoType Graphics.

First Edition
Manufactured in the United States of America.

Table of Contents

I
Addiction 11
Marginalia on our Bodies 13
Numbering the Thunder 15
Before I Begin 16
I'm Not Vishnu 17
Life on the Prairie, Continued 18
Notorious 19
The Midway 20
Miners on the Prairie 21
The Left Bank 22
Never, So Long 24
How I've Missed You 25
A Souk Of Any City 26
The Way Back 27
Life on the Prairie 28
When You Come Back 29

II
The Book of Isaac, Burning 33
    Coming In 33
    In the Heaven Before Night 35
    Anonymous Annunciation, Circa 1450 36
    On the Outskirts of the Lost Cities 37
    Visited 39
    The Past Described, As a Figure 40
    The Daughter Tells of Her Dream 41
    What Isaac Knew of Forgiveness 43
    The First Temptation 45
    After a Father 47
    Vertigo 48
    Opposite the Angel 50
    On the Imperfections of Messengers and Similar Instruments 51
    The End of Sacrifice 52
    White: Echo 53
    After Abraham Mourns, He Requests Another Son 54

III
Postcards from the Holyland   59
Where Is It Written   61
Out of Nowhere   62
Before We Are Raised   64
With All We Have   65
After a Grand Silence   66
Before Alexandria   68
On Your Retreat   69
Ulterior Summer   71
Hearing of the Astronomer's Death on the
    Road Home from Moorhead   72
Closing Time   73
The Evangelist, At a Distinct Advantage   74
First Body   76

To Therese

I

I find a relapse unto my old symptoms as I wont to have it many years ago, as after sleeps; strife at meats, strangeness, clouds, etc... Strangeness in beholding darksomeness, offer to groan and sigh.
— Francis Bacon

Addiction

The pumpkins rotted, poisoned
by slow rain. Kneeling
in the garden, locusts chant
their bitter hymns,
beating spears against
the black shields of their wings:
    They sing against
the winter.

From the middle
of the prairie, it's half
a day to the Forbidden City.
The other half
is dust.
    Now that you have eyes,
now that you've seen,
you're certain
you've been shadowed,
        maybe somehow
cared for...

And your people, what
did they know? They were closing in,
dying for a glimpse, the tell-tale
crack.
    They gather round, whispering,
  and wonder what it's like,
the burning.

The endless jobs were mindless,
if you can call that easy.
How the center was a wind
    not moving,
everywhere. Snow
geese ride

their white road south –
that was good to see again.

Beyond that,
she covers her face
because you will leave again, wrecked
and filled by a breeze,
a rush igniting the upsweep
of your neck.

That's the first thing you feel –
breath. How you turn suddenly
and see the trees
just finished moving,
      and if you could speak
it would be for everything
    to be as it was.

Marginalia on our Bodies

Not that evening, early, when
we begged for retro-rockets to slow
the turning of the moon
to mud, or the bitch
star to light the grounds
of new rendezvous, oh we liked it —
the selected pleasures
of that modernity.
I especially remember
secondary relics: the rasp
of your lips, saliva, the salt
flat of your belly.

Now we slip
toward vespers, singed
by a slight twist
of vodka, humming
in the clear velocity
that shoots us past
the nights when I was plausible,
and yours. Here we sit with snapshots,
nodding, pretending
to remember our regret.
                              Or, work
to work all over, in the following
light. We bank
on restoration by dinner,
an annulling thump of hunger...

and search again at midnight
on the cliffs
of your bare torso
for the scrawled marginalia left fading,
words we wrote, in tongues
and lip, into the vellum

of our younger skin. Beneath
your breast, I find crude
Sanskrit praising the gods we left
and the gods that left us,
singing.

      In the last night,
when workers come to gather us
as we were, they'll see
   the scars used to mark
where we'd been hurt
on skin brilliant
and eternal as tattoos.

Numbering the Thunder

Sitting in a single canto of torchlit May,
earlier than the insects, almost spring,
I'm not sleepy. I'm not anything
but outside, semi-alert to pleasure
inside of a day that will soon be forgot.

And then the clouds come, the air green
in a pre-tornado stupor, the baby crying
at the calm, the pressured hiss. The eye
of the storm stalls around us, bringing
sulphur to the surface of the skin.

All the windows are shuttered, the chores
finished earlier, the bed made up cleanly
in its room. I look into the distant city,
patient beside my wife. We count together
after lightning: First the broken barn.

Then the cold. Then the gathering in.

Before I Begin

To start again beneath the grille-
work of branches; that is,

always to begin. Waking, to see the wind
matting the pines, now bent to the West

and tomorrow. Our children are filthy
and we salute as we pass

the evidence of today's kitchen,
awkwardly worrying a key passage

of Bach to death. That chord
of geese keeps thrumming

overhead, beating a runway
to water. We haven't been kind

to our muscles – grouchy, anxious
to be touched another way. We baked

half a day on the unforgiven
beach: it's not smart to peel

your chest, it's too soon.
You swell in the night, banked

in hot folds, the sprawled children.
I'm itching to take off your skin

and touch you to see which I want more,
to be burned or to be the burning.

I'm Not Vishnu

My friend knows a man who's
famous in India, starring as Vishnu
in a Madras soap opera.
My friend's friend thinks London
is the only place for vacation
because there, he says,
"No one thinks I'm Vishnu."

I know the feeling. Today,
a washed-out spring day
not good for much, I'm glad not to be
Bacchus or the Buddha, it's a relief
not to be Mark, the Son of God. It's good

to be out wasting time, shaking
my head over the junk the neighbors
dropped in our yard. They smile
as they pass by the house
and they wave and I wave
and they wave. I smile as I say
to the back of their car, "Father,
put out their eyes," and they wave
and I wave, nothing's happened.
There's no recall to Rome,
cardinals kneading their hands,
there are no sirens, no schisms,
no coups. *Stick it up your ass*, I sing,

and kick around my yard. Everything's
fine and I'm getting by, no more
divine than that bird over there,
whatever it is, and no less.

Life on the Prairie, Continued

We've come to to a scarcity of ocean and
admire so much – the high relief
of mountains, an aroused sense of lilacs,

the heifer's benign stare – we lose track
of what we sacrifice. Why do we stay
when we didn't build these phony sets

and we know the carpenters were drunk?
We pitch our tents on temporary plains,
billed as former mountains. You can see

the mainsails rising in the wheat. It's flat
enough to find your body where you left it
last night – just thread your hand through

the finger holes and flex. Prairie lore
suggests it's traditional to lay out attractive
magazines, to fashion an ethnic waiting room.
You understand, it's customary to wait.

Notorious

At the end of the evening famous for never
ending, where we stand together, unable
to remember, I saw her, here, at the very

end of darkness, where it turns tawdry,
shrunken at the seams. Who was she then
or now, my overweight teacher is furious

to know, how dare she be elusive in the way
she loves: liar, diaphane, weisenheimer.
The eye's amused by lying. And so

it sees. How rude not to deceive me,
refusing to rearrange her face into another
burst of French, a feint, her notorious grin.

She puts me on, naively, in her first tongue.
Now I'm certain she and I go way back
in the dark. I move to close the book,
her face. We open it instead.

The Midway

The software's incredible, while the light
dissolves behind our heads — the Midway.
We coast on an unlimited sequence
of yes and not-yes which gets us
where we're going. The darkness
deepens as we travel the electric divine
into an implacable mind, moving at the speed
of thought. We see ourselves as children,
playing in the lit alcove above the water.
We don't know each other yet
and you see how she learned to be
alone, how she practiced holding still.

She sees you spear your brother
with a rake, skip school, hitchhike
to Montana. We're both twenty-three
in a crowded barroom, sitting
in adjacent booths, laughing, arms
around our first loves.

The way it works is you meet,
you fall so fast, you marry,
the children walk into the room.
You see yourself eat dinner
in the spring. You've never noticed
the trees, so huge, waving outside
the room. I see my Pythagorean wife,
made of numbers, of notes, break
some celery in her mouth, watch her eyes
watch the children talk, rest her head
in her outstretched palm. It's early
evening. Her shadow stretches
across the floor. I don't know
that I can bear to know her better.

Miners on the Prairie

For isn't that what the Old Ones
have always called us, their dogs,
their Saxon whores? The imaginary

"We" who come behind, haggard,
bloodied, swallowing what we're told:
the earth's a spitball hurdling through
a lecture hall; the topic? Hermeneutics.

It's been hinted a small handful
of the living know the ropes, hand-fed
by Teutonic experts. They worry –

if I were the last man on earth
would I know enough to turn
the lights off when I'm done?

Who do they think they're kidding?
Where I come from we're used to it.
We do our best work in the dark.

The Left Bank

Lying back in beheaded wheat,
the stalks gouge your side
in the middle of this bad and ruthless
harvest.

A cicada burns August into an idiot rhyme,
a hot whine
gauging the heat. Off to the left,
the lake evaporates,
heat lines rising,
the far shore melting through
summer's mirage.

Halfway here a mouse
dropped into the center
of the windshield, materializing out
of the rotten wicker
seat of the canoe.

It looked right at me,
eyes widening going 50 down
a dirt road, shit quickly,
then jumped off
when I slowed.

Now a yellow-jacket
keeps sliding off
a sweet bud of clover.
It climbs back on,
humming to itself, smeared
with pollen, smashed.
I'm frightened of you.

As we make love for the first time
outside, it's as if I'm not there.

I rest my head
on the drops of sweat
still clinging to your breast
and hear your heart, roaring
like a hive. The child inside
is listening, waking
particle, bare
and partial wave.

I feel my own heart drumming
on your arm, answering,
amazed.

Late that night
I shower, my chest
still swarming. Explain it
as a box of bees,
a whirring spiral
rising like the mayflies
by the lake today. The insect cloud
recalled a face, formed
by wings, turning in a fog.

Or explain it as a mob
of mice, a single-minded
mass of lemmings.
Across the bottom of my heart
I feel a soft stampede
of padded feet, the clammy
track of cold black tails.

      Darling, do they act
  as one?
Or does each one
size up the sea,
and jump…

and how do they know
who stays behind?

Never, So Long

It is no mercy to have lived your life.
All I want is what you've seen, falling
through. You never sent word but

I knew you had crossed here, knew
you were with me. I've been quiet
and clever, afraid always, until

I heard you had been here before.
You never lived. You lived just
a matter of hours, you've been hidden

though I did know your voice. They never
spoke of you. A pinched moon breaks
in the window, days after Mother died.

I found a Certificate of Live Birth
in her old photographs, dated two years
before I was born. I knew you
when I saw my own name.

How I've Missed You

I clamored for you, drunk
on the statue's glamorous wounds

and made my eyes burn, praying
to the lip-shaped gashes.

"Strip us, Oh Lord," the congregation
prayed, "Of all our sins."

"Strip us and rape us, Oh Lord,"
I mouthed because I knew

the gods visited from time to
time and we killed them

or they changed into barnyard
animals and slid into bed laughing

because now their wives wouldn't
recognize them and who knows

maybe I too could wash their feet
with my hair, afterwards.

A Souk Of Any City

What will I call you, brother, before
I send you off forever? I call you
mine but not yet me. Stripped cord,

odd lot, you fake hunger, mumming
for the widows. I know you want
nothing, are nothing, suffer a fallacy

of pain. Put my envy aside; you'll always
need my yearning. You need me pleading
to be peeled from my wet suit, hovering

close to those I love. No wonder you're
distant — my clinging is so crude. No wonder
you're dead. I'll ride with you through

the market of Tyre, oh, any holy city just
until I press my face against the children's
sticky shoulders. Until I know that you won't
lift me. Until what you lack is all I need.

The Way Back

I'd be more guarded if I knew you were
watching, leering, nearly naked,
stylishly at rest.

You're wrong if you think I want to be known
utterly, you in your angelic homburg,
fogged in reticence.

I talk to myself in our own olden tongue.
You hear I know by the quality
of your indifference.

I rave about the others, halted on the road,
insist we've not conspired —
You ride alone.

I know what you like by the way that you
leave me. We're never going
back, are we? Speak to me
one more time about home.

Life on the Prairie

Why do we stay here, sleeping on a dwarf
dream, the subtitles shaky, waking to fish
for loose change? I'd like to go inside now

where it's warm and you never know
what's next. Under the Big Top
of my mobile home, a survival kit's

included. It's a real time-saver, what's more,
it works — I'm spared the spectacle
of the chapped, you know, the portable

sky. Inside we have our own dome, sugar
doughnuts, and the outline of an escape.
I don't find that comforting. But it beats

sleeping on the knife. The meadowlark has
just one song. Clearly, we hear what we've
missed. I live here anyway, in a landscape
shaped like it's impossible to end.

When You Come Back

And what of the nights you visited
the boys, laying hands above their eyes

to mark their dreams with smoke
left in their throats. Coughing

they woke to a glimpse of your twisted
silhouette, turning away in the closet.

You're gone so I went to meet you
in the shocking sun of Main Street

all the scorched, last year of that survival.
I read day for night all night and still

the thrill, how it tore inside me. Somehow
I got through, trying not to.

And then I came back. Not as the dead
return in dreams or a sick child in a miracle

woken by a word — I came back
as you walk across a field.

II

The Book of Isaac, Burning

The Book of Isaac, Burning

> *I will let him come freely into my presence*
> *and he can come close to me;*
> *who else, indeed, would risk his life*
> *by coming close to me?*   Jeremiah

1. Coming In

Before this life,
there was another, so
convincing in its ignorant display
of rain and lowlands
we thought it might
go on forever. We were
mistaken, in fact,
forgiven, you see, in that life
we were young.

    Now nights
my son wonders
what was here before he came,
I could tell him
it was March. I remember
pitted snow,
the rotten roads.

For weeks the prairie sky
was the dead-color of clay
gashed by firelight – flames
from the distant
burning cities, remember?

There was a turmoil in the broken snow

fields, like the narrowing
in the coming night. He is young, once
I was young and from the slim
candlelight of late dinner
he became.
 Red, red the opened mouth,
shaped-valentine – laughing,
and then he came.

2. In the Heaven Before Night

    Inside the end
of the walkway, entering
dusk, she stood bordered
by blue vines, floating
   in the sky
of the reflecting window.

    Lover,
and the children
   to be born
sit outside the evening, one
already there in the cold air
that battered in our chests
as we got him,
    made him
one of us – then spoke
of other things
separate in the dark.

3. Anonymous Annunciation, Circa 1450

In scrolled *aves*
and erect
seraphic wings,
no one notices,
at first, her eyes.
You see
she is from
Siena.

Lapis lazuli,
however rare,
must be used for
her abrupt blue
royalty, while also
adequate
(if you look
far enough
into the violet
funnel
of the eye)
for fear.

4. On the Outskirts of the Lost Cities

~

That the wandering
would be the more-favored part,

this was unexpected, exceptional.
Even the gnaw of the harness,

faces shawled
against the dust, nights

without fire – sweet to him now –
even this.

Who could find that point again,
at the canvas steppes

where exhaustion forced them on
into the serrated mouths of grass

rather than return
to what they knew,

the lush blur
too thick to show the way they came.

~ ~

That when they couldn't go on
that place looked like every

other place, but now
familiar. Where later the trees bent

like wind stopped in mid-breath
that would make him miss the wandering.

That the children and their children
would flourish, then sicken and die

very near here, he'd known that
in stopping – it was always implied.

This only meant they cherished
the fields of their hunger, their dirt

and why they spoke, instead,
of joy. Like the hymn he sang

praising the road that took him
from the walls where a son finds himself

staring out from his father's face,
separated only by years and anger.

5. Visited

There's joy for the well-turned
shin-bone, praise for the wrought
torso, we were warned
      when he opened
those gray eyes.

      What gifts we gave
we gave for virtues — a white stone castle
to teach him courage, small guns
to set the blood. A storybook,
illuminated, kept him close, hard
against the fire.

      He was prone
to broken sleeps, rifts with milk,
a rude, colicked baby, satisfied
in solitude. Knit of slurred, imperfect
purpose, he's come to dream. After-
math, blood puppet, my salvation,
dream has come to dream.

6. The Past Described, As a Figure

What were those days like? Remembering
is like remembering

white, or water. It's another resemblance,
the libraries packed

with broken metaphors, book after book filled
with "water is like...",

"white as..." When Alexandria caught fire,
the librarians burned like candles,

like suet. As for the manuscripts and their similes,
nothing was lost – it was like a fire.

7. The Daughter Tells of Her Dream

Once in the smoke,
you got a sister
and we ran away.
This was before
my eyes caught fire,
and the choosing,
before the bread was torn.

Of course we were caught.
Then we were threshed
and laid straight in the furrows,
this was before the harrowing.

If we lay still as a stone,
we might be safe. No one
told us our fear
would be the children's
favorite part
of the story, later.

Already my feet,
your feet were up in the air,
pulled swinging from our crates,
set upon the floor.
Birds with kind faces examined
our bellies, we laughed
at the tiny bites.

The nursemaid descended
from her patch in the desert,
slapping the stones from our hands.
Everyone knew she ate the bread
one by one.

At the choosing, the old man waits

wearing the striped robe we touched
at night, worked in fox fur
or mink, the clean smell of horse,
liniment, myrrh, the v of the beard
I wanted
to touch, to touch me.

He was taken straight back
to the woods. I called in my mind,
run brother, run Isaac. Branches
criss-crossed on a pile, the sun
glared on the stone like a knife
shines before it cuts.

A voice from the tree became the tree.
Now father returns, leading
the sheep and each night as we lay
in the barn, I put my mouth
behind his ear, repeating
Father loves you.

8. What Isaac Knew of Forgiveness

He counts on me
like he counts the corn,
worrying down to Harvest.

While Father sleeps,
the moon gets fat on cheese.
It lasts all night,

her little head on fire,
still eating. She's like me,
I heal well, too.

When Father leaves for town,
there will be a silver
flask, forgotten

cigarettes, everything
I've been punished for
there for the taking.

In the morning I still like
to see the thorn riding
its rose

and put out
my thumb to prick
the needle, swollen to the stem.

When he returns, the mare blooded
on the flanks,
I'll clear her eyes with water,

then vapor seethes off her back.
The mare is so beautiful
he rides her

too hard to get home, the way
he loves me so much
it makes him angry.

He said I am forgiven.
I only have to ask like the bird
for seed. I'm the one

who caught it and named it,
stupid wren crashing
into windows. I only expect it

to sing. I give it old cake
drenched in honey, stick
his beak shut, say *Sing*.

9. The First Temptation

Strangers came across the plains
as gods

to barter. Strangers or gods,

they were soiled, mindless
as children,

bandaged.

Helmets black and white, wings filthy,
some said

divine. They come to parley, set
the ransom.

So they could leave.

We open the doors, throw corn
on the floor,

Let the gods eat.

They took our stores, drank our wine
and left

the women alone, black eyes

like stone. So
holy,

experienced. The old ones, relieved

the gods had voices, nod
when a priest says he knows

their language:

*Give up
what you love most*

and you are not alone.

No one had dared hope
for the suffering

we could choose.

The gods are always with us
as strangers,

as birds.

From high on the hill, I watch
them

leave as geese,

braid into the clouds
with their cry,

Give up, give up...

Down near the river, my son slips
through the reeds,

thin arms, back bare,

sliding
through gray cane.

10. After a Father

There may be justice
in retribution, but it isn't

human – it seeks a mouth
to give it lips, then laughter,

the full sorrow of a mortal
face. In this short life, the wound

is verified by the knife. And so
a father will pull his son

behind him like a plow, and how
a son will lodge against the rock

to break his father down,
the taut reins hot and singing.

In the wake, gulls circle,
crying like misers for the seed.

A father will drive his son
into the burned ground

like a post where he leaves him
to learn patience, he leaves him

the opened field,
the laughter of the birds.

11. Vertigo

As if falling
would be enough
    as in
surrender
      as if the antidote
to fear
is fear
      refined,

you give yourself
as nothing
      to the armless effigy
   of submission
and falling
is the prayer,

rushing face-
down in a mesh
of rain and ordinary
air, speed
lashing eyes
to slits, drifting
in certain aspects half-
asleep

Wanting it, teetering
on the edge,
between falling
and crawling, back taut
against the arc
of the almost-fallen object,
backwards against
the need just
to get it
over, the wind

forced against your nostrils
as breath

But he
is not to fall
ever before me
I rush to the hunched-up body
his knee bloody
beneath the tree

I turn his small face
see he's fine
and slap his mouth shut

This is what fathers do
I say in the empty
tunnel of my body
though I don't know
what fathers do
though the tunnel
is caving softly
and the last air
rushes slow

12. Opposite the Angel

I was ignorant, waiting for your body.
Ignorant, unnoticed, I waited for you.
Black temple of open eyes, black meadow
of matted hair, I waded in the water,
stumbled out to reach you, to bring you
into shelter.

This time, not in anger, I take you
in my arms as if you were a little child,
lay your throat bare. His messenger
is upon me,
          now I must take you
out of love. You'll no longer suffer
the grinding wind.
            When you come to me
    we'll ride so fast
you won't suffer at all.

13. On the Imperfections of Messengers and Similar Instruments

They say that when God speaks,
He speaks in flames:
what you know
is burning.

When He comes to you,
your brain on fire, think you

could fill us in:
      what kind of god
would know your name,
would say it
        and not destroy you?

   This one burns
your mind, enters you
while you sleep
in smoke.
      He has His way
   and you fake-moan
as He fingers inside your fur,
tracing the fine-tooling
of your saddle.

So spit it out, speak
in tongues, for christ's sake tell us
what we're supposed to do…

But you don't know Greek or shit,
      the tongues
of God are licking you
and you can't say a word:

All you know is
burning.

14. The End of Sacrifice

Stitched up with gut-string, sinew,
        into the woolen skin swaddling
        his body, still warm,
        the boy is curled
        at my side, as though sleeping.

He was the end of life
        as he was the sum.
        He held more than the river
        its banks, and then
        more.

Take him up, the last cold thing,
        across the stone circle,
        lay him down
        once.

The air is smoked razor-blue,
        and cuts down to the skin. Smoke
        billows up the body, glazing
        the outsides black. All
        is burned, all burns
        away, burning its
        own hole.

When I walk down off the mountain
        I'll carry the ram across
        my shoulders like
        a shroud.

As they turn toward me, they'll look
        right past. They'll never
        see me as
        a man.

15. White: Echo

As white shutters and as white
As tourniquet,
As black
As creeks,
As numerous
As glass, the window shattered,
      kindly, to save the fist
As groan, as famine feeds thin dogs, the father falls
As pinetrees into pitch, as tongs
      hammered into sleep so hard you can't stand it,
  that's what dawn is.

After the candles gutter,
after the hall,
after the shut door, the hesitation,
the shut door
shut.

After the son dies, fathers.–

After the son dies.–

After a son dies a father
is no father. When
the father is strong enough
to dig the grave, they
won't let him. He is strong enough
to lie down and they won't let him.

Sit here, they say, but he won't let them
help him. Help him.

16. After Abraham Mourns, He Requests Another Son

Off day, the prairie sill
at evening, choked
    with mustard,
thistle, the coarse meadows
failing
at twilight. Then father

went out. To see
early stars turning
    on their bitter
wheel, the small flames
making the lowland
evening blacker.

I'm old, he said
    to the night,
alone with the women.
They're weak, they can't
    keep these lands.
In winter they'll eat the corn.

Then God scattered the skies
    with father's seed,
and commanded him
to care for each one.
    Count them
and when you tire of counting,
that number will live for you,
    will suffer
in strange lands,
will lose the way.

Dead, they will be yours.

Then father fell to the ground,
weeping, but God said

*You can't give these
sons back to me* and went away
the way a father always
leaves a son,
        mercifully,
while my father sat in the dirt,
chanting His name.

III

Postcards from the Holyland

Isis waves from an Umbrian
window, probably
toward the cypresses which flicker
and turn before
the hooded gaze

of W. H. Auden slouched
in a New York daze of snowflakes
at St. Mark's Place.
The funereal bar, Dublin
I suppose, shows a sign for Guinness

and spirits served. At the bottom
of the bulletin board,
a grim Joyce strums
a toy guitar
partially covering my friends –

a detail of Margaret
in the mountains
(the Cascades at eight) –
next to the neighbors
as Salvador and Gala Dali:

The Florida Years. A quick
glimpse of the Pyramids,
the holymen eclipsed
by a poem of Rimbaud's
near a torso of Joe,

hands blurred, and in a few
months he'll be dead.
Now he hammers,
the angle toward Delphi.
At last, a haloed old woman

holds up Jerusalem.
The abandoned, the ignored,
I know them. The cast-off,
the disregarded
are mine, too. They're saved,

but somewhere else, not
in the Portrait Hall
of nostalgia.
The failures of other times
are lost in air –

the heat in the summer
of fabulous lies,
the cloud of rain
when I turned away.
Now I ask good fortune

for the judges, all those who
took my side. While
it's true I sold
our teacher to the guards,
they know

I didn't do it
for the purse of gold:
all I wanted
was the recognition
and the kiss.

Where Is It Written

The signs were clear in autumn, not just
in your eyes, on the battered land

and the rough day bed. Fall rain came
to no purpose. Beneath the eaves, we eat

pot-luck while the children discuss their future
pleasure without us, how the furniture

will be arranged. We've argued against
tomorrow, which the Czech bus driver

said we missed, which is all I know
about this pressing in my throat

that doubles as fulfillment, near
fulfillment, made sharp by hope with

an after-taste of silver, like a syringe.
I can change. I can hope for change.

I can mark the spot beneath the graphs
of stars where we built the small houses,

the montage of aspen and the paths through,
but. As the stars give out in the morning,

I ask *Does this look familiar?* – the white,
connected rooms where we live.

Out of Nowhere

Now that you're not dead
again, but swollen
on intelligence
of those you've called
the other ones,
is that you I see, skinny
in the distance
hobbling off in glamour?

I'd thought we'd go
together, tipping
lavishly, a bit off-
center, as we slipped away.
But that was years
ago, now we'll find
our own way there.

Now that you're not dead
again, you dodge
sideways into the slow
breeze, to merge into the blue
fresco behind the beeches, sitting
in the chassis of the clouds,
brooding, you think
picturesque.

But I hear our
friends down South
have seen you stitched
against the backdrop of your new
kitchen, leaf-
prints in the bathroom
where you look
into your eyes,
hypnotizing your hair

into the cottonwoods
of the farm. You said you told
the suicides you would live, but why
should we care. You've never
used words the way
we do. What does
live mean this time
to you?

I wait for your trip up North
to stand outside buildings,
smoking, walled inside
the blue exhaust of our
breath. But yes we believe
you will live. We're
just waiting for you
to say where.

Before We Are Raised

The dead choose
the kitchen table to return to.
    A year later he appears
with a fruit jar of water, head
down. "It's hard," he says,

"Much harder than I thought."
    She imagined death
as a restoration,
the one body falling away in a ditch,
    but this other, couldn't
his torn neck be mended,
the fingertips repaired?

He should come back
head wreathed in Buddy's music, blue
notes trailing like drugged mosquitoes,
    his wounds smoothed in.
But here he comes,
caught wearing an old grin
from the one face
    she knows is no longer
his face.

    She finds his lost glasses,
she sees the dog-eared page and hears
    the mosquitoes whine
their old song, broken
bow on a broken violin.

You can hear it in the night
when sleet rips the road
    when the dark body inside the body
returns to ask for water.

With All We Have

When I'm nothing beneath the tree,
skin burned in memory of the sun,
lasting the greater part of Tuesday
in relaxed and ample ignorance

When I have done enough to lay
my glasses down, and, with all we have,
look at nothing, stop my mouth
pile the books on the other side

When I'm done with birds and fields
and curve my arms behind my head
and am nothing beneath the tree
when I have given all I have away

And the swamp is distant, faintly whirring,
the loose-strife's purple clinging
to the weed, before I leave I watch
the white air work its damage in the trees.

After a Grand Silence

I expect the
garden to gleam
more and to yield
redder flowers

too. Yes, I've thought
of a lake where
foreign friends glide
laughing about

perfections of
summer. Ours is
not like that, more
ordinary

usually.
But the spirits
wish we knew them
better, you say

they speak always
like gnats buzzing
in our ears, there
before we fall

to sleep, thinking
again that we're
alone, a child
or a stone, say,

with nothing else
to help us but
nothing there to
keep us from just

sleeping. We'll hear
bees whirring in
armor, the hum
leading others

back from lilacs
to the hive, re-
turned to the sane,
inverse flower.

Before Alexandria

There is always the river and then a rise
from a white bed. Trees turn to elders
limping at night, singing through cleansed

streets, the night-scent of needles. Out-
riders play as shadows on the parapet
to punctuate the rain. By this I mean

memory. I asked *Will I remember this?*
When what I meant was *When will it end?*
Troy burns endlessly in the library

so the pictures stay the same, always
burning. The river guts the lowlands,
then gives way to the sea.

Bracken burns in Turkey, boats
are lowered for new books. The elders
look for me: I'm hidden in the bedroom,
pages like smoke in my hands.

On Your Retreat

I take it your joy is neglected or
you take it neat, on your own.

This matter of waking, furiously,
in small throngs… maybe instead

of preaching, you should quit
sleeping with the choir? But it's habit

that makes your body appear
speechless, between the hours:

you notice yourself
at work, at rest, laughing

with your bologna sandwich.
And why not? All the nations rejoice,

the caddis flies possessed in their rise,
needing once to be lit together by dust.

But don't dwell on it, we have no
need to be reminded of their luck.

It's bitter enough to rest.
I know we sat in houses and lived

awhile with ourselves glimpsing
the eclipse through a pinprick, tense,

surprisingly muscular, armed for God-
knows-what. I envy you not saving

yourself the trouble of a broken heart.
Now don't waste your time divining

the second guesses of Freud, The Bearded
Lady of Longing. Just say hello to our

mutual friends on the road. I'm still nosy
about your losses, the odd-jobs on the way.

I even envy you weeping as you bathe
the old women. When you speak to them

in a whisper, you find that they have gone.

Ulterior Summer

Escape was by sea,
we were delirious in clear

water, bug-eyed
at the slow chromatic

explosion beneath
the bay: the extremities of coral.

The hills were dredged
in laurel, bay, the grave,

dried olive. I swam
back to the raft

my hand red with coral
to amaze you

and surfaced seeing
you and our son

alone while I
floated toward you

remembering what it was like
not to be there.

Hearing of the Astronomer's Death on the Road Home from Moorhead

In the immense condensed zero
he said we'd survive —
a half beat of music
darkened by debris
from a sun. Along
the fine lines of jigsaw cuts
that compose the scrolled moment,
aisles of Red River cottonwoods
sway in smoke — farmers burn
back the weeds near the rye.

Eternity may not be too long to be gone;
we'll remain a tune
the children can't get out
of their minds. With a rise,
I leave the floor of the prairie,
and pass a gray coat forgotten
on a post near West Union. Poplars
shake yellow hands down,
my eyes confuse
the leaves with the tree.

Closing Time

There's time to get lost
driving the low hills north of town,
navigating by ear: I steer west
from "Respect" for Aretha, then north
by Patsy Cline.

There's a third eternity slipped
between the two others, lit
from without, just as brief.
The disced fields ignore
the red river, roar through Manitoba
while late static clogs the radio
and the car stalls,
backfiring under Cassiopeia.

Enlightenment's wasted on the enlightened.
When it settles like those pigeons
on the humped barn in St. Wendell,
I quit humming, think,
"Check the oil?"
And it moves through St. Wendell
where Donnie smiles as he chooses
the last lottery number,
where Marlys brushes
her daughter's hair into a wave.

When the radio's back at 5:00 AM,
the Dalai Lama sings
through B.B. King, sweet licks
of moaned Tibetan blues. He means –
see the corn at daybreak.
It's all there, this
is where you've been.

The Evangelist, At a Distinct Advantage

Divinity is contagious,
some sticks to me,
like dust, or
drugs. It drips down,
slow as love – dumb
and second-hand.

I was His favorite. He preferred
me to eternity. But He
was painted in. I pain
not. Nor shall I pant,
or want. I am nothing
but a word.

     I suffer
not, I turn from nothing
I want, and in this way I look
impartial, I serve him better
as His imperial tool.

       In time I will relate wonders.
If He so inspires me,
with wonders.

On the walks by the sea,
I'm not fasting:
   I'm waiting.
I can wait
for the better food.
If there is no wine,
     we'll be given wine.
If no bread, fish.

What will they do
with the extra fish? Gutted,

the lips gape,
mouthing *glory, glory.*
      Bury them,
and the lettuce
runs wild next year.
      The smell
on your hands stays
like He said the soul stays
      behind, a stench
you're never rid of.

First Body

May and the great trees rage,
white sap burned up
into leaves. Turn
and beneath the branches see
   the actual air
moving, hesitant, green.
     This is when the soul knows
it has a body,
   by wanting
to leave it.

In the morning, bowed
under blue rain, geese beat
their heavy way back
   to the city-state
of mud. Rising, the wings groan,
   trying to fly away
from the body.

     Winter
was hard, the cold broke
weak and strong, together. Stay
   and watch the robins scream
over scattered barley.

   This is how we came to
love this life –
   by wanting
the next.